"What ever happened to that other guy?"

WHAT WOULD SATAN DO?

Cartoons about right, wrong, and very, very wrong

BY PAT BYRNES

HARRY N. ABRAMS, INC., PUBLISHERS

"Why, that's an outrage. Just who do you think you are? Me?"

INTRODUCTION

We like to think it's easy to know right from wrong. But in the heat of real-world moral decisions, things often arise that cloud our minds. Emotions, desires, talk radio. Perhaps it would be less difficult if we had better contemporary role models. After all, it may do to choose a car or hairstyle based on celebrity endorsements, but can you imagine the chaos if we modeled our everyday actions on them? Not even Jerry Springer could endure it. So we are told to consider, "What would Jesus do?" But who the hell knows what he would do? Jesus simply didn't do enough in that Mel Gibson flick for us to predict. I mean, you couldn't use that to program a video game avatar's actions, let alone provide comprehensive life instruction. If, on the other hand, we were to ponder, "What would Satan do?"—ah, now we're talking. Answers start raining down like frogs in Egypt in that movie with Yul Brynner and Charlton Heston. But how is that any more useful than asking what celebrities would do? A compass that always points south can help you find your way as surely as one that always points the other way. Likewise, a moral compass that always points to the wrong pole can be just as useful. If you know what would absolutely be wrong, then you know that you should absolutely search in the other direction. Still, no matter which way your moral compass is magnetized, even your best attempts to navigate by it may have been thwarted from time to time. All you can do then (some would say it's your moral imperative) is to look for the good to be gotten by reflecting on your humiliating missteps. For instance, take me. I have gotten a book out of it and, I hope, will profit greatly by mocking the spiritual struggles of others. Oh, and you will have gotten a few laughs. Laughter being good for the soul. And all that crap. And . . . Oh, who the hell cares? Where's my royalty check?

"I got a call today from the forces of evil. They're asking me to join."

"Remember, we can only afford to do all this pro bono because of how much the anti bono pays."

"What's our policy on honesty?"

P. BYRNES.

"Look, lady, we're not bad people, we're just really lousy at what we do."

"Harper has raised a concern about the perceived dehumanization
of our organization. Any thoughts before we devour him?"

"Hey, if it's a corner office you want. . . "

"I won't be giving a sermon today, because you're all going to hell anyway."

"Oh, great. There's a line."

"Sure, there's the endless torture, fire, and shrieking terror. On the other hand, there's lots of nudity."

"Hmm, what would Satan do?"

P. BYRNES.

"To ten happy years of marriage, which is pretty amazing considering the other twenty-two."

"Eighty-five dollars, just to poke my head through the door! Doesn't that make you sick?"

"I'm all in favor of approximately equal rights."

"Oh, good. It's someone important."

P. BYRNES.

"You lost because you didn't hate hard enough."

"The speeding was only thiry-five dollars. The rest is Ticketmaster."

"Sorry about your kid, lady, but I'm outsourcing now, and the dingos were the lowest bidder."

"After sending all those jobs overseas, it only seemed fair to do the same with myself."

"I answer only to my shareholders."

"Don't tell *me* about busy—I'm on my freaking honeymoon."

"What would Jesus do? I'm pretty sure he'd go with the five iron."

"My folks are so cute. They're from that generation that had morals."

"I'm never sure—how much do I tip?"

"Put a trace on this call. He's asking if the sex offender registry is for gifts."

"He'll confess, but only on *Oprah*."

P. BYRNES.

"On the bright side, a life sentence won't leave you with any future savings concerns that might interfere with your paying my bill."

"Please listen carefully, as your rights have changed."

"Just remember, son, it doesn't matter whether you win or lose—unless you want Daddy's love."

"It's so refreshing to meet a man who's good with children."

P.BYRNES.

"We finally realized that morale among management is important, too."

"'Release the hounds.' That's your answer to everything."

"Don't talk to me about sex. My generation invented sex."

"Remember how I said my dog ate it and you said that was no excuse?"

"Stand down. It's only toxic waste."

"We felt it was important to talk to them about values while they were young, and get it over with."

"Here are the ads, or, as we like to call them, weapons of mass consumption."

"Relax, we only want to cannibalize your culture."

"When I lost my sense of humor, I lost my sense of compassion, which is how I got where I am today."

"My business school reunion's tonight. Don't wait up."

"The question you have to ask yourselves is, did the police do all they would have done on *CSI*?"

"It doesn't count if it's in a salad."

"Put that résumé away. With some people you can just tell."

"Yes, I went down a long tunnel. Yes, there were family members waiting
for me at the end—but they were all in-laws."

"I'm only here until vindicated by history."

"I still say it was worth the lifetime free tech support."

"You couldn't put on a tie?"

P. BYRNES.

"It will be nice to have children, so we don't have to take out our moods on each other."

"When you said 'Big Bang,' I thought you were loosening the rules on sex."

"The way I like to look at it, today is the last day of your past."

"You understand, of course, this isn't strictly legal."

"At worst, my client is a wrong-doer—by no means an evil-doer."

"When push comes to shove, we simply can't afford the luxury of ethics."

"You have the right to a judge. If you cannot afford a judge. . . "

"I had to settle for the participant-ribbon wife."

"I don't want to treat you like dirt, but I don't want to lose you either."

"I'm sorry, Tommy, you've been voted out."

"The reorganization is fairly straightforward."

"It would be sad if he wasn't so damned cute."

"I'm sorry you're not feeling well. Maybe it'll help you to focus on *my* problems for a while."

"Our HMO won't pay for stapling."

"I just want her to be a happy baby. That would show those bitches at the park."

"My wife told me to work on my faults, but just how much more does she think I can drink?"

"Ooh, I'm sorry, my mistake, sir. That sign *was* meant for someone with a less expensive car."

"Give me a quarter, I'll hail one for you."

"It's perfect—all our friends will hate us."

"My next car, I want one of those."

"I wish I wanted more stuff."

"Researchers say that I'm not happier for being richer, but do you know how much researchers make?"

"Surely they realize that ethics laws just put us on the slippery slope of legislating morality."

"I hardly had to pad my résumé at all to land that job as ethics officer."

P. BYRNES.

"I was comped."

RATIONALIZATIONS 50¢

P. BYRNES.

"See? This should ease your conscience. He's an organ donor."

"But if mommy and daddy don't both work all the time, how can we afford to buy your affection?"

"This is all your fault."

"They're letting me erase my debt by declaring moral bankruptcy."

"It cost me everything I once held dear, but you can't put a price on money."

P. BYRNES.

"Mister Jackson! You know how I feel about sampling."

"But what if that guy in the bleachers is right? What if I do suck?"

"She loves you not, so back the hell off."

"I can't help thinking of the lyrics to that old song *I Want To Sex You Up*."

"Good God, Gloria! Just how many guys have you been with?"

"What ever happened to the public's right not to know?"

"I wish there'd be another anthrax scare, we have such a perfect graphic for it."

"What role did sex play in the earthquake?"

"Let me through—I'm curious."

"He's so assholier than thou."

"Look, I may not have much so-called experience, but I *have* watched an awful lot of television."

"Hold on! You can save up to 50 percent on emergency costs by dialing 10-10-911."

"It's just a release for *Funniest Home Videos*."

"Where's your helmet?"

P. BYRNES.

"Your nanny is *paid* to be patient with you."

"Ah, well. Such is the price of freedom."

"It's just a little rash. Rub some stem cells on it."

"Can't we simply agree to both be in the details?"

"This one comes with the 'Entitled Driver' package."

"300 times the salary of the average worker may be what the average CEO gets paid in this country, but you're not paying me to be an *average* CEO."

"I just need you to go in there and chum the waters."

"*Think* outside the box, Peterson, don't *go* outside the box."

"On a date? You wanted me to take your sister out. . . on a date?"

"Put the punster in with the mime."

"Sure, it's a nuisance lawsuit, but it's not a frivolous lawsuit unless the nuisance isn't big enough to draw a settlement."

"I took my husband's name, but only for the sake of credit card applications—just before the divorce."

"Not to be judgmental or anything, but who are you to judge?"

"Don't worry about it. I'll pay them back when they catch my cold."

"What? They're recyclable."

"It's low-carb."

"I know how much you like this movie. It's not due back till Wednesday."

"I'm okay with the message of non-conforming, as long as it's going to make everyone buy our product."

"Do as I think, not as I say."

"So you won't take 'No' for an answer. Then how about 'Burn in hell'?"

"That's why we stopped taking Texans."

"We ought to get back and go to bed soon. The guys are all in town and
want to shoot some hoop in the morning."

"Which tie says, 'I met a younger woman and I want a divorce'?"

"Of course I know you're downsizing. That's the job I'm applying for."

"I thought I was being ironic when I suggested that."

"See? You had a problem, and you spoke up about it. Now doesn't that make you feel better? I hope so, because you're fired."

"Maxwell, I want you working on that idea of yours. The rest of you, drop everything and find me some reasons why it won't work."

"Turn in your apron, Kenny. Corporate's bumped you up to Marketing."

"I know it's tech support, but for $2.50 a minute, I expect you to talk dirty."

"This jerk is deliberately doing the speed limit!"

"An out-of-control news van mows down fourteen people on a crowded street
this afternoon. Channel Six is first on the scene."

"His only real mistake was admitting a mistake."

"You can't legislate morality, but you can sure as hell legislate against it."

"I'm losing my faith in cynicism."

"There's real money to be made in selling anti-consumerism."

"Hang on, let me call up your file."

"Does this make me your bitch?"

"You wasted a whole week on *that*?"

"It's from one of my old students saying she's forgiven me for ruining her life."

P. BYRNES.

"Do you even *care* about evil anymore?"

Editor: Harriet Whelchel
Editorial Assistant: Isa Loundon
Designers: Brankica Kovrlija and Neil Egan
Production Manager: Steve Baker

Library of Congress Cataloging-in-Publication Data

Byrnes, Pat.
  What would Satan do? : cartoons about right, wrong,
and very, very wrong / by Pat Byrnes.
      p. cm.
  Includes bibliographical references and index.
  ISBN 0-8109-9243-4 (pbk. with flaps : alk. paper)
  1. Right and wrong—Caricatures and cartoons.
2. American wit and humor, Pictorial. I. Title.

  NC1429.B92A4 2005
  741.5'973—dc22

                                          2005009000

The author would like to acknowledge
and thank one of his magazine editors,
Bob Mankoff, for continually pushing
him to evolve as a cartoonist; his agent,
Linda Langton, without whom this book
would be a clutter of paper in the
author's office drawers; and his father,
Patrick Byrnes, for decades of encour-
agement and support. And, of course,
the fine folks at Abrams, for being so
bold as to tackle a project like this.

Printed and bound in China

10 9 8 7 6 5 4 3 2 1

Harry N. Abrams, Inc.
100 Fifth Avenue
New York, N.Y. 10011
www.abramsbooks.com

Abrams is a subsidiary of

LA MARTINIÈRE
GROUPE